To Herman, a dog of uncertain origin, but for whose love, affection and continual presence at my feet this book would have been finished a lot sooner

Also by Stephen Baker:

5001 Names for Cats
How to Live with a Neurotic Cat
How to Live with a Neurotic Dog

Games Dogs Play

Stephen Baker

With illustrations by Jackie Geyer

GRAMERCY BOOKS
NEW YORK

This 2006 edition is published by Gramercy Books, an imprint of Random House Value Publishing, a division of Random House, Inc., New York by arrangement with McGraw-Hill Book Company.

Gramercy is a registered trademark and the colophon is a trademark of Random House, Inc.

Random House
New York • Toronto • London • Sydney • Auckland
www.randomhouse.com

Printed and bound in the United States of America

Interior book design by Stephen Baker

Library of Congress Cataloging-in-Publication Data

Baker, Stephen, 1921-
  Games dogs play/Stephen Baker; with drawings by Roy McKie.
    p. cm.
  Originally published: New York : McGraw-Hill, c1979.
  ISBN 0-517-22743-6
    Dogs—Humor. I. Title.

  PN6231.D68B29 2006
  818'.5407—dc22

                                2005045628

10 9 8 7 6 5 4 3 2 1

Contents

1

How Dogs Have Become That Way: A Candid Look at Canine History

To UNDERSTAND the games dogs play and why they play them, we must first of all understand canine psychology. "But that's impossible!" the majority of dog owners will say.

The majority of dog owners are absolutely right. This, however, should not keep the rest of us from trying. Actually, a dog's way of thinking is not nearly as obscure as might be surmised from his actions.

In fact, all canine behavior is motivated by a single desire: to obtain the basic necessities of life—food, sleep and a scratch or two under the chin—while exerting as little effort as possible. Perhaps a quick glance at the ancestry of the modern dog will give us some insight into his way of thinking, if that is what his mental process can be called.

It is generally believed that the dog was the first animal to be domesticated, getting ahead in this respect of the sheep, the horse and the myna bird. This is an intriguing theory but one that does not hold up under close scrutiny. The simple fact is that dogs have never been domesticated.

Nor is there any indication that they ever will be.

Domestication is clearly not what dogs had in mind. No self-respecting canine is going to play second fiddle to a mere *Homo sapiens*. At times he may put on a convincing performance to sustain that illusion, but that is only for his own practical reasons.

The truth remains that it was *not* man who discovered the dog. Rather, it was the dog who discovered man.

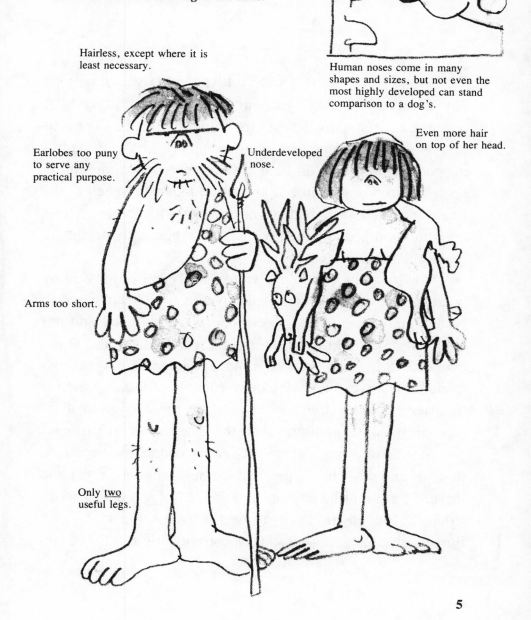

Prehistoric people—as seen by the dog.
Their physical and mental faculties
appeared to be inferior to most—possibly
all—other creatures living at the time.

Hairless, except where it is
least necessary.

Human noses come in many
shapes and sizes, but not even the
most highly developed can stand
comparison to a dog's.

Even more hair
on top of her head.

Earlobes too puny
to serve any
practical purpose.

Underdeveloped
nose.

Arms too short.

Only <u>two</u>
useful legs.

WHAT HAPPENED was this: One day about ten thousand years ago a pack of wild dogs was roaming the flatlands looking for something to eat. The animals were as tired as they were hungry, since they hadn't napped in more than an hour. It was then that, quite unexpectedly, the dogs came upon an odd-shaped species, the likes of which they had never set eyes on before. These creatures walked on their hind legs, apparently trying to make themselves look taller.

At first glance the dogs were not all that impressed by what they saw. Their newly discovered friends appeared to be singularly inept. They were poorly coordinated and not even as good-looking as their closest kin, the apes. However, the dogs soon found out that appearances can be misleading. The creatures were quite capable of looking out for themselves. They lived in caves, ate regularly and slept through most of the night. And they had invented garbage.

It was not long before the leader of the pack realized that he and his colleagues had come across a very good thing. That night he approached the cave for a closer look. When he poked his head inside, he was astonished—and immensely pleased—by the accommodations. Lined up against the walls were comfortable-looking bunks. The creatures inside were sleeping under animal skins, with only their heads and toes exposed to the elements. Then and there the leader of the pack decided on a bold course of action, the first of its kind in the chronicles of man–dog history. Ignoring the cacophony of snoring that assaulted his ears from all sides, he stepped over the sleeping bodies and worked his way across the cave. He found what appeared to him the largest of all covers. With a gentle shove he sent the cave man beneath it sprawling to the floor. The snoring stopped and the creature sat up, rubbing his eyes. Trying to recapture lost ground, he then clambered back into what he felt was his exclusive territory.

All this activity prompted the dog to make another important decision, the second of the night. Resisting his natural impulse to bite off the man's nose, he licked his cheeks instead. The result surprised him. A slow, silly grin spread over the countenance before him. The cave dweller patted

his new bedfellow on the head and allowed him to take over more of the space—roughly 80 percent. Without a grunt of protest, the cave man contented himself with the remaining 20 percent.

A historic precedent was set.

Dog had his own reasons for joining the human race. Such an arrangement provided him with 1) a roof over his head, 2) a steady supply of garbage, 3) tools that took the work out of hunting and 4) such sleeping conveniences as a pillow and a blanket to keep him and—possibly—his human companion warm.

ADDRESSING the pack the next day, the leader related the events of the night before. His colleagues listened with rapt attention. They could not fail to recognize the significance of his message. It did not take them long to make up their minds.

After the meeting, they decided to scatter in all directions. Each dog selected a "master" bearing this important qualification in mind: He had to be the owner of a blanket large enough for two, or at least large enough for the dog.

This marked the beginning of one of the most beautiful and touching relationships that has ever existed between man and an animal. From that day on, dogs would share everything with their owners—beds, meals, automobiles, living-room couches and, finally, television sets.

In the early stages of any relationship, a few misunderstandings are bound to develop. Dog–man relations proved to be no exception. First there was the matter of hunting. It had occurred to the cave men that dogs could take part in tracking down wild animals. However, they failed to consider that this would require some effort on the dog's part as well. Fortunately, as time went by, man discovered the error of his ways, and he and his dog resolved their differences. One solution was to have the dog hold absolutely still— "freeze"—at the sight of the game, thus saving himself from over-exertion. Another was to have the dog trap, rather than chase, the quarry. The third—which proved to be the most popular with the dogs—was for the hunter simply to leave the dog at the campsite with the women and children and bring the dinner home himself.

Still another controversy arose between man and his dog when someone proposed having the latter pull loads along the ground. This idea immediately struck the dogs as unsound. No dog is fond of traveling on foot, let alone being mistaken for a beast of burden. Man had little choice but to find other means of transportation, such as riding on horseback, on snowshoes and, finally, in an automobile. The last solution has especially appealed to dogs. Not only did the automobile relieve them from having to walk from one place to another, but it also offered them the opportunity to sit back and think.

As the years passed, man's understanding of his canine friend has much improved. He has long since stopped making unreasonable demands on his companion. In return, dog has lent man his bodily presence—and nothing more if he could help it.

Today, dogs have finally reached the status to which

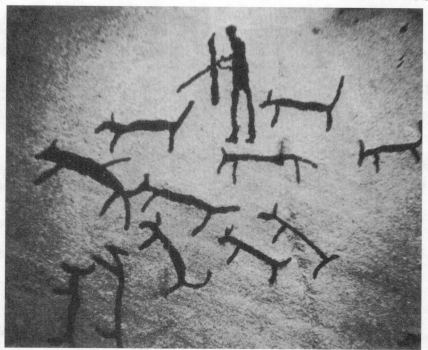

**Drawings of dogs appear on the walls of prehistoric caves, as in this
one discovered at Multane, France. At the top of the rock painting
the Bronze Age hunter can be seen straining his bow and arrow.
He is surrounded by a group of dogs, who, quite typically, are all
lying comfortably on their sides, probably sound asleep.**

they have for so long aspired. They have become ''pets'' in
the true sense of the word. To a dog, the dictionary defini-
tion of this term is so satisfactory that, if it were up to him,
his owner would recite it daily. To wit: PET. ''A domesticated animal kept for *pleasure* rather than utility'' (italics,
dogs').

Intrigued by the close companionship that has developed between man and his dog, artists have frequently made
it the subject of paintings. Although the owner's pose varies
from painting to painting, that of the dogs does not. They

11

Terborch, Gerard, The Music Lesson

Pierre Auguste Renoir: Madame Charpentier and her Children

Sir Joshua Reynolds, Portrait of Miss Bowles

are invariably depicted actively pursuing their favorite pastime—resting.* Trying to make dogs' lives more tolerable, man has invented a vast number of energy-saving devices. Shown here are some of the most outstanding ones from the dogs'-eye view.

Not all inventions represent progress. Three that have incurred the permanent wrath of dogs are 1) soap, 2) the Murphy bed and 3) the garbage compactor.

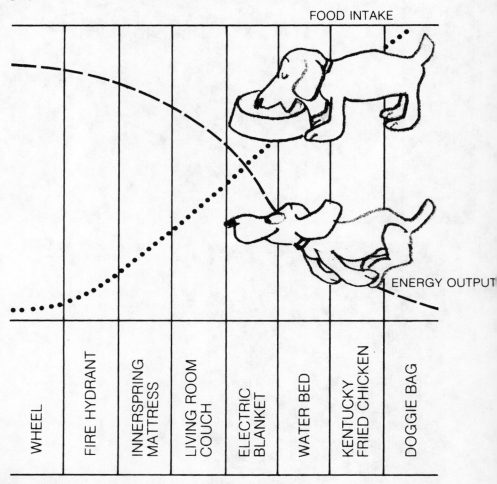

FOOD INTAKE

ENERGY OUTPUT

WHEEL

FIRE HYDRANT

INNERSPRING MATTRESS

LIVING ROOM COUCH

ELECTRIC BLANKET

WATER BED

KENTUCKY FRIED CHICKEN

DOGGIE BAG

* In all fairness to the dog, one ought not conclude that he sleeps *all* the time. He most certainly does not. When it comes to food, for example, dogs have been known to open both eyes, make a special effort to leave their owner's bed and follow the scent unerringly all the way to the kitchen.

THE MODERN DOG

Dogs have changed a great deal over the years. For one thing, they no longer look much like dogs. Canines these days come in a variety of shapes, sizes and colors. Each breed is designed to suit the animal best to the kind of owner he wants. As of the writing of this book, the American Kennel Club recognizes 124 breeds of dogs, with several more insisting that their bark should be heard.

Dogs come in three main sizes: 1) small, 2) large and 3) too large.

To avoid confusion, among both dog owners and dogs themselves, attempts have also been made to classify dogs by—for want of a better word—"function."

HUNTING DOGS

Greyhounds
Egyptian Greyhound
Indian Greyhound
Saluki
Afghan
Irish Wolfhound
Scottish Deerhound
Borzoi
English Greyhound
Whippet

Hounds
Saint-Hubert Hound
Mastiff (Alan)
Talbot
Pyramus
Foxhound
Bloodhound
Vendean Griffon
Basset
Beagle

Gun Dogs
Italian Spaniel
Irish Setter
English Setter
Cocker Spaniel
Field Spaniel
Braque
Pointer
Bloodhound
Curly-Coated Retriever
Chesapeake Bay Retriever
Owtcharka
Spanish Spaniel
Irish Water Spaniel
Gordon Setter

Sprinter Spaniel
Norfolk Spaniel
Wiemaraner
German Pointer
Golden Retriever
Labrador
Otterhound
Elkhound

WORKING DOGS

Guard Dogs
Tibetan Mastiff
St. Bernard
Newfoundland
English Mastiff
Brabant Mastiff
Bordeaux Mastiff
Boxer
Great Dane
Doberman
Schnauzer
Keeshond

Shepherd Dogs
Pyrenean Mountain Dog
Persian Shepherd Dog
Old English Sheepdog
Bouvier des Flandres
Alsatian
Collie
Shetland Sheepdog

Terriers
White English Terrier
Wire-Haired Fox Terrier
Welsh Terrier
Kerry Blue Terrier
Scottish Terrier

Bull Terrier
Staffordshire Bull Terrier
Boston Terrier
Dandie Dinmont Terrier
Airedale Terrier
Smooth-Haired Fox Terrier
Irish Terrier
Bedlington Terrier
West Highland White Terrier
Cairn Terrier
Skye Terrier
Sealyham Terrier
Corgi
Dachshund

Sled Dogs
Samoyed
Alaskan Malamute
Husky

PET DOGS

Italian Greyhound
Chihuahua
Dalmatian
Aztec Sacred Dog
Miniature Spitz
Pomeranian
Yorkshire Terrier
Poodle
Bulldog
Little Lion Dog
Tibetan Aspo
Maltese
Pekingese
Japanese
Pug
Schipperke

In the opinion of the majority of dogs, however, the chart on the left is needlessly complicated. It creates the wrong impression among today's dog owners. Closer to reality would be the chart below.

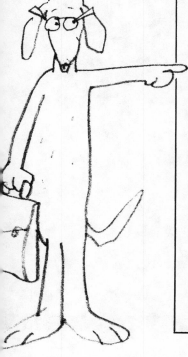

NON-WORKING DOGS

Greyhounds
Egyptian Greyhound
Indian Greyhound
Saluki
Afghan
Irish Wolfhound
Scottish Deerhound
Borzoi
English Greyhound
Whippet

Hounds
Saint-Hubert Hound
Mastiff (Alan)
Talbot
Pyramus
Foxhound
Bloodhound
Vendean Griffon
Basset
Beagle

Gun Dogs
Italian Spaniel
Irish Setter
English Setter
Cocker Spaniel
Field Spaniel
Braque
Pointer
Bloodhound
Curly-Coated Retriever
Chesapeake Bay Retriever
Owtcharka
Spanish Spaniel
Irish Water Spaniel
Gordon Setter
Sprinter Spaniel
Norfolk Spaniel
Wiemaraner
German Pointer
Golden Retriever
Labrador
Otterhound
Elkhound

Guard Dogs
Tibetan Mastiff
St. Bernard
Newfoundland
English Mastiff
Brabant Mastiff
Bordeaux Mastiff
Boxer

Great Dane
Doberman
Schnauzer
Keeshond

Shepherd Dogs
Pyrenean Mountain Dog
Persian Shepherd Dog
Old English Sheepdog
Bouvier des Flandres
Alsatian
Collie
Shetland Sheepdog

Terriers
White English Terrier
Wire-Haired Fox Terrier
Welsh Terrier
Kerry Blue Terrier
Scottish Terrier
Bull Terrier
Staffordshire Bull Terrier
Boston Terrier
Dandie Dinmont Terrier
Airedale Terrier
Smooth-Haired Fox Terrier
Irish Terrier
Bedlington Terrier
West Highland White Terrier
Cairn Terrier
Skye Terrier
Sealyham Terrier
Corgi
Dachshund

Sled Dogs
Samoyed
Alaskan Malamute

Peg Dogs
Italian Greyhound
Chihuahua
Dalmatian
Aztec Sacred Dog
Miniature Spitz
Pomeranian
Yorkshire Terrier
Poodle
Bulldog
Little Lion Dog
Tibetan Aspo
Maltese
Pekingese
Japanese
Pug
Schipperke

ANATOMY OF THE PRESENT-DAY DOG

In keeping with the laws of evolution, today's dog is superbly adapted to his environment. Each part of his body plays a well-defined role in the daily struggle for survival. The purpose of the tail (**1**) is to be able to create a quick favorable impression on onlookers by wagging it. His nose (**2**) enables him to sniff out nearby food, a prospective mate or a human being without having to open his eyes. His four legs (**3**) carry him from bedroom to kitchen and back. A little-known (though often observed) fact is that dogs, much like giant constrictors, are able to store up a large amount of food in their belly (**4**) so they can stay alive for long periods of time between lunch and dinner. Inside his head (**5**) there is some evidence of a brain (**6**), an organ whose function is so far not fully understood.

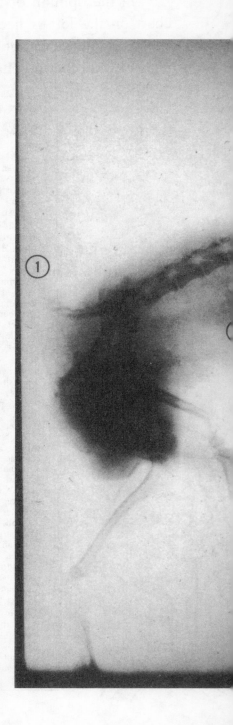

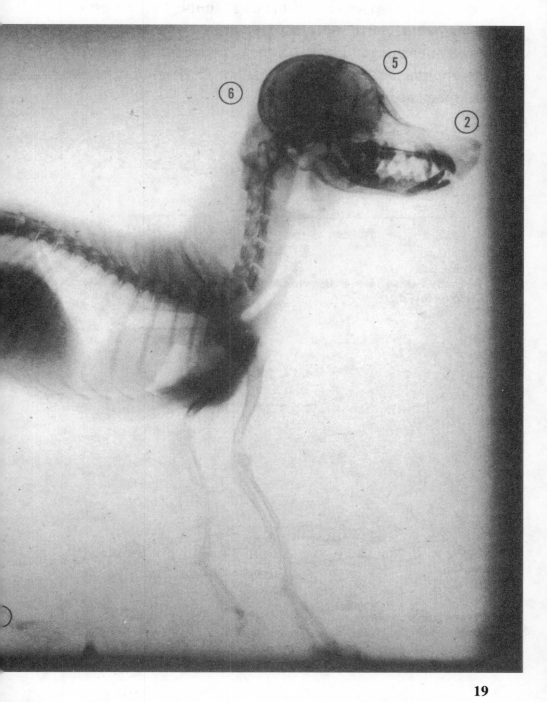

19

As we have mentioned, man is still trying to improve upon the original version of the dog. To this end, he uses a technique he calls "selective breeding." The technique is aimed at creating a dog that is perfectly adapted to his present environment, a well-furnished home. Here are some of the more successful permutations.

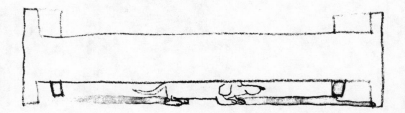

Dachshund
His body is slung low to the ground; this breed fits under most any piece of furniture.

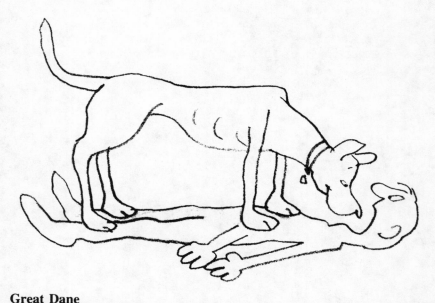

Great Dane
On his hind legs, a full-sized Great Dane towers over most people. His size and weight enable him to make his presence felt under any circumstances.

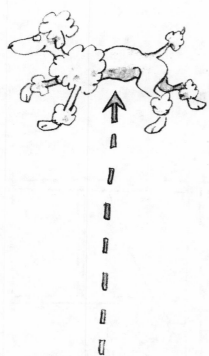

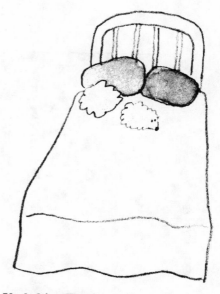

French Poodle
Having perfected the vertical take-off from a stationary position on the floor, this dog can easily reach the top of any bed, dresser or pantry shelf.

Yorkshire Terrier
The key to this breed's success lies in his superb camouflage. His round, compact body, covered by a white fluffy coat, often causes the owner to mistake him for a pillow. Thus the Yorkshire Terrier's chances are better than most that he will not be removed from the top of the bed.

Old English Sheepdog
His face hidden by fur, this dog's fore looks exactly like his aft. Only his hairdresser knows for sure whether a sheepdog is coming or going.

Dalmatian
Protective coloration makes it possible for this breed to avoid detection in certain rooms by positioning himself next to the wall.

2

Why Dogs Think People Are Crazy: Canine Con Games

Owners MAY HAVE

difficulty understanding their dogs. On the other hand, dogs have no trouble at all understanding their owners.

As far as dogs are concerned, people are basically very much alike. Their wants are simple. To wit, all people:

1) need affection
2) think they deserve it
3) demand respect
4) think they have earned it
5) wish to be popular
6) see no reason why they should not be.

Keeping this in mind, a dog has no problem getting his way. He knows that deep down his owner is anxious to please. As a matter of fact, dog owners often make better household pets than their dogs.

It takes the average dog only a few weeks to find out the truth about his master. Education begins early, as parent dogs explain to their offspring what they may be

up against for the rest of their lives. Each generation then adds its own experience to the information pool. This process of learning clearly provides the answer to that often asked question: What makes today's dogs so knowledgeable about people?

Some puppies begin their study of humans at the pet shop as they watch the crowd gather outside the window. Pretending to be hard at play, they can observe their future owners make fools of themselves in every way. They wiggle their eyebrows up and down, stick out their tongues, smack their lips, tap dance, blow kisses, froth at the mouth, snap their fingers, clap their hands, press their noses against the glass and otherwise try to prove that underneath it all they have a sense of humor.

Owners come in many sizes, shapes and temperaments. Ask any dog.

Six reasons why dogs think people are odd:
1) They eat off tables, not the floor
2) Their bathrooms are not equipped with fire hydrants
3) They eat only when they are hungry
4) They normally go for several hours without napping
5) They actually seem to enjoy taking baths
6) They scratch dogs and cats but seldom one another

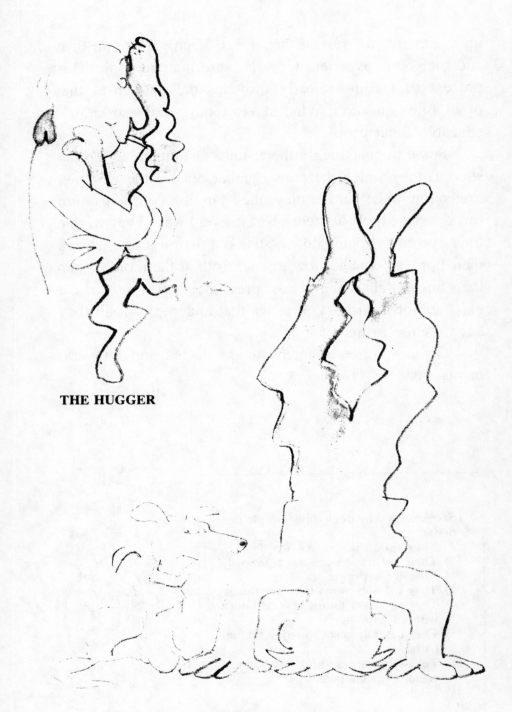

THE HUGGER

THE PLAYMATE

THE TALKER

THE SHARER

30

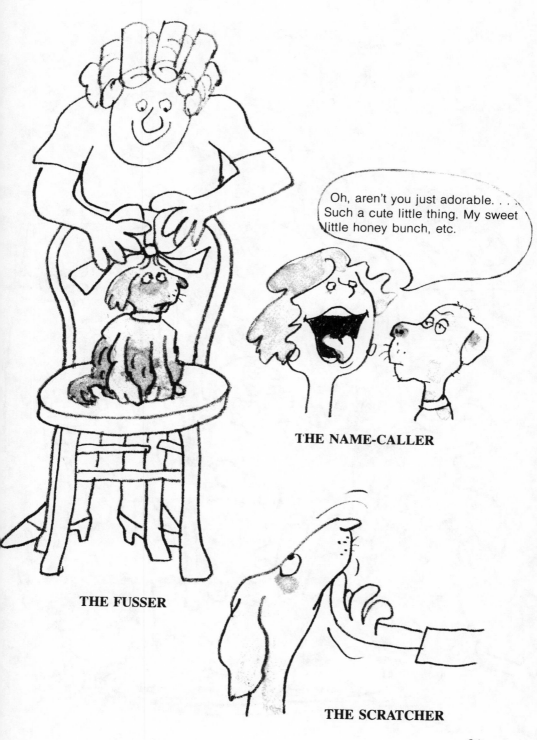

THE FUSSER

THE NAME-CALLER

THE SCRATCHER

31

No ONE KNOWS better than a dog how to make his owner feel more important than he is. All dogs are shrewd psychologists, superb negotiators and believers in compromise, as long as they come out ahead. If necessary, they will even try to humor their masters. For example, when a dog is told not to eat off the dining-room table, he will oblige by finishing the same meal on the kitchen floor. Or if his presence in bed appears to interfere with his owner's sleep, again the dog has the perfect solution. The owner can move to the living room and have the whole couch to himself.

Dogs realize that in return for room and board they must give their owners the sense of being loved. To accomplish this, dogs use a wide range of techniques, all of which have one thing in common: None requires much if any, effort on the dog's part. Still, these techniques are very effective. Invariably, humans refer to them as "endearing qualities," which is exactly what the dog had in mind all along. Listening to his owner's praises, he chuckles to himself all the way to the feeding bowl. Shown on the following pages are just some of the more popular techniques dogs use to make an impression on people.

Horses and cows wag their tails too, but people are hardly impressed.

Many centuries ago dogs found that tail wagging—an exercise originally devised to scare away flies—is interpreted by humans as a sign of hearty welcome.

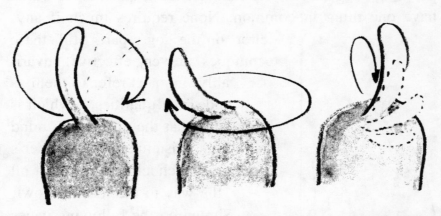

Through the years, dogs perfected a variety of movements with their tails. Tails can be made to move on different planes, depending on the dog's inclination (1 and 2). Some dogs are able, by dexterously combining up-and-down and side movements, to draw more or less perfect circles in the air with the tip of their tail (3).

34

Up-and-down tail movement can be observed with dogs resting under a blanket—which is often. This indicates dog's willingness to share his sleeping quarters with his master and should be taken as a friendly gesture.

The sound of drumbeats resulting from his tail hitting the floor is a frequent source of amusement for dog, if not for owner.

Sideways movement of a large tail requires plenty of room—whether or not it's available.

Some dogs use their eyes to create an effect. The "admiring glance" calls for raising the eyes, following the master as he stands up. The "sidelong glance" is calculated to leave owner with the impression that his commands are closely heeded. Half-shut eyes give dog the appearance of listening thoughtfully while allowing him to continue with his nap.

Most dogs are willing to shake a hand offered to them. They find, however, that it takes far less effort to let owner lift the forepaw for them than have to raise it themselves.

DOGS HAVE LONG come to recognize that the one thing that most impresses masters is their proverbial loyalty. The word has a nice ring to it, and it's associated with a sense of high moral purpose. In this department, dogs have a distinct edge over, say, horses, cats or pet alligators, all of which may be just as eager to stick around but don't seem to have the know-how. No one, for example, ever talks about a "one-man alligator."

The average dog will do everything he can to maintain the image it took years to achieve; he's smart enough to know that this can do him no harm. He may go so far as to run away from home on occasion, knowing that absence makes (human) hearts grow fonder. He knows that when he shows up again, after a few hours—or days—the much relieved owner takes this as another sign of his dog's devotion. All is forgiven as the dog heads toward the kitchen to soothe his pangs of hunger.

A kiss from a dog is the highest form of flattery—or so it seems to dog owners. It can be planted on or near (1) the cheek, (2) forehead, (3) nose, (4) mouth, (5) under the chin. A variation of the kissing game is licking. Licking consists of up-and-down motion of a very wet tongue—a technique invented by the ant-eater and further refined by the dog.

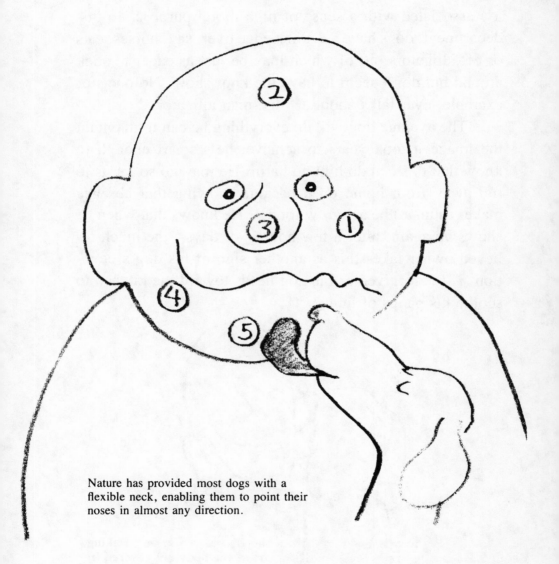

Nature has provided most dogs with a flexible neck, enabling them to point their noses in almost any direction.

The Morning Kiss is commonly given shortly before owner's waking time. It can be firmly placed on any part of the body not covered by a blanket.

The Good-night Kiss is basically the same as the Morning Kiss.

The Continental Handshake should always be accompanied by a kiss. The tradition was begun in Europe by French poodles, spread to Italian greyhounds and from them to Bavarian schweisshunds. Today it is widely imitated all over the world by dogs minding their manners.

The Jump Kiss is another surprise greeting used mostly —but not exclusively—by smaller breeds. It consists of leaping jumps in the general direction of the face. Smack on the face is delivered on the way down.

40

3

Ancestral Games: "The Beast Is Back"

Ten THOUSAND years is hardly enough time to change one's ways—certainly not as far as the dog is concerned.

Fundamentally, his attitude is still that of his progenitors, except that today he no longer feels compelled to chase after his dinner. It is put before him, or, better yet, he is invited to share meals with the rest of the family. This gives him more time for peaceful reflection.

But even amidst this life of leisure, the average dog cannot—and will not—forget the call of the wild. Age-old savage instincts still stir deep inside him. Fortunately, your home—or, more accurately, *his* home—provides just the right setting to relive the past, find the enemy waiting for him and generally act out aggressions he has held back, sometimes for hours at a time.

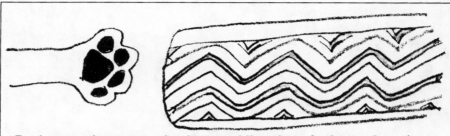
Dog's paw—its texture closely resembling that of a heavy-duty tire—is built for making fast stops on a floor.

True, he may find his movements restricted by such man-made contraptions as walls, doors and large pieces of furniture. But none of these is enough to stop him or even slow him down. Once in motion a dog can hold his own, not only on the ground but high above it. Wings or no wings, he has no trouble flying over couches, chairs, tables and people in beds. Or—if the need arises—he can work his way from one side of the room to the other by tunneling under the carpet. It is said that some dogs are even able to scale walls —a throwback to the ancient practice of stalking mountain goats up solid rock cliffs.

The speed at which some dogs can—and do—cover distances is one of the miracles of nature. Many owners maintain that among all animals, the *Canis familiaris* must surely be the swiftest of foot, leaving behind such noted per-formers as the gazelle, the cheetah and the common cock-roach. Once, rumor has it, a medium-sized mutt was abruptly awakened from his 5-hour afternoon siesta in the bedroom by the scent of pot roast reaching him from the kitchen at the other end of the house. He was clocked at just over 100 miles an hour in covering the distance between the two points just before he took a six-foot slide on the freshly waxed linoleum floor to avoid crashing into a table leg.

Some owners go as far as to claim that their dogs move faster than the speed of sound. While this has yet to be substantiated, the fact that some dogs are able to materialize in the kitchen before owner has finished calling their names lends credibility to the claim.

For reasons known only to himself, the route a dog takes, unlike the bee or the crow, is never a straight one except at mealtime. He is inclined instead to take the most circuitous way possible, bobbing and weaving in and out of the furniture which happens to block his progress. This practice also has its origins in prehistoric times. In those days, zigzagging was a way to confound the enemy.

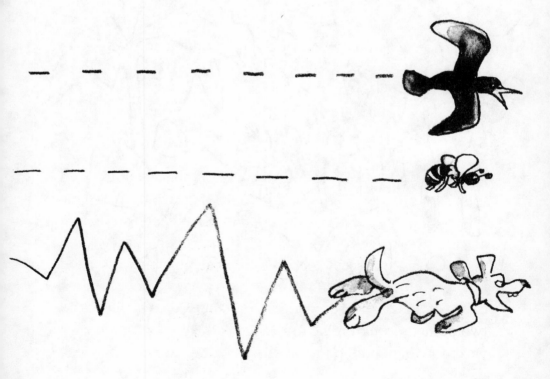

46

Dogs have developed the uncanny ability to cover a distance of several miles in the living quarters of their owners' home—and all that in a single burst of energy. Shown here is a typical running pattern of a dog.

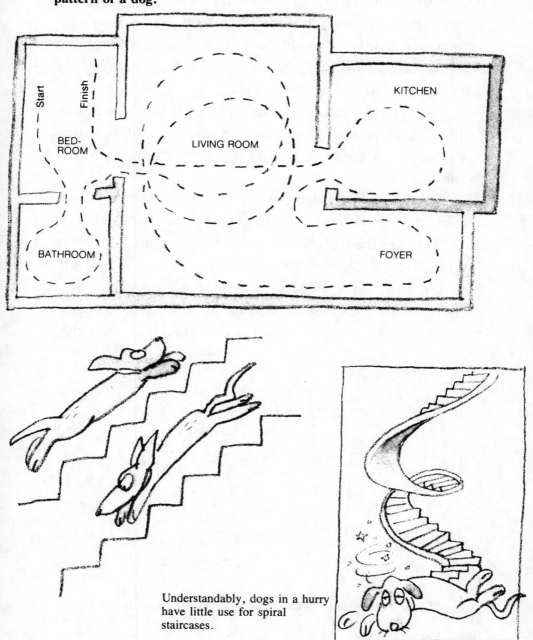

Understandably, dogs in a hurry have little use for spiral staircases.

EARLY DOG enjoys making use of his most formidable weapon—i.e., his teeth. As a puppy, he goes through a period of teething during which he particularly enjoys chewing on things. This penchant for chewing may persevere through his entire puppyhood, usually lasting from ten to fifteen years.

This should be no cause for alarm. Gnawing is a perfectly natural activity with dogs. Remember, if he bites down on one of your hands, you still have the other to dial for an ambulance.

This is not to say that dogs will chew on anything they can lay their mouth on. For example, when it comes to a dish of food, they prefer to swallow the portion whole, regardless of its size. On the other hand, they will take their time chewing such objects as a pair of Gucci loafers, leather-bound books—Shakespeare is still their all-time favorite author—pillows, cigars, nylon stockings, automo-

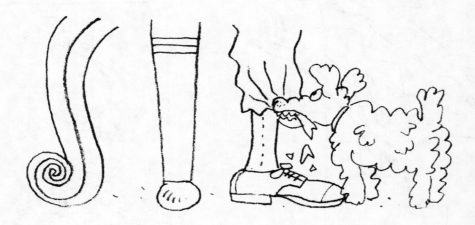

Legs—of any kind—are a special target for dogs moving in for the kill, and, as far as they are concerned, for good reason. In primeval times, the quickest way to stop a bigger animal was to go for a leg.

bile seat covers, towels, electric extension cords and Sunday newspaper supplements. The purpose of chewing is not to appease the appetite but simply to enjoy a sense of power.

Owners are often puzzled as to why dogs feel compelled to bury objects in the most unlikely places. This habit also can be traced to dogs' forebears.

Going around in circles before finally settling down is another canine ritual of ancient origin. It was one way to check out the lay of the land.

Dog getting ready to take a nap at noon.

Dog getting ready to go to sleep at night.

It IS only natural that a dog should jealously guard his "territorial prerogatives" against all comers and most of all his acquisition-minded peers. This is particularly so when the other dog happens to be smaller.

The boundaries of every dog's domain are exceedingly well defined, at least in his own mind. They usually mark a sizable piece of real estate several blocks long, or—not infrequently—the entire city. Among his chattels he numbers the beds in the house, the linens, the carpeting and the furniture—in short, the entire house.

For the record, dogs will leave their "markings" at certain carefully chosen locations. Fire hydrants were invented for just this purpose. They are designed to accommodate both short and tall dogs and are painted flamboyantly to make them visible from a distance. Moreover, in order to give canine pedestrians ready access, city ordinances wisely prohibit parking in the immediate vicinity of fire hydrants.

Still, it is not always clear which hydrant belongs to whom. This is especially true in a city heavily populated by dogs. Territorial disputes are usually settled in a forthright manner—i.e., the dogs take each other by the throat and refuse to let go until pulled apart by the owners. Each dog will then go on his way, taking a piece of flesh with him in his mouth as a trophy. Both will then continue to look for the next challenger, probably just around the corner. Dog will protect his territory not only against other dogs but against *all* trespassers.

Here, each dog claims half the city as his territory. As is often the case, the two territories overlap. In Manhattan alone there are about a million dogs with similar notions. 1) Poodle's territory, 2) St. Bernard's territory, 3) Combat zone

Human babies are a source of joy to their parents but not to dogs. Babies, too, demand constant attention. Who needs that kind of competition?

Vacuum cleaners are so noisy they stop dogs from being heard.

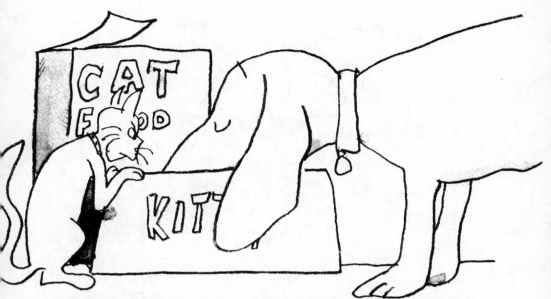

The greatest problem with cats is that they like to eat, just like dogs.

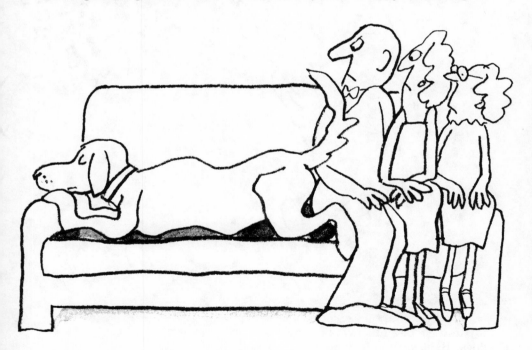

Guests take up room.

**Looking out for No. 1: Life would be so much more pleasant if only
there were no other dogs around.**

4

**People Games:
The Training
of a Dog Owner**

Dogs LONG AGO discovered that of all living creatures, their owners make the best playmates. Not only are they easy to have a good time with, but it takes very little to make them laugh.

This is fine for dogs; they too enjoy doing things just for laughs, as long as the last laugh is theirs.

However, when it comes to playing games, people have certain limitations. They are handicapped by their size, poor muscular coordination and lack of imagination. Most are reluctant to get down on all fours to be on the level of their canine playmates. Nor are they particularly skilled in jumping over obstacles, digging tunnels in the ground, rolling over or barking.

Nevertheless, most owners deserve credit for at least trying to stay in the game.

What makes people such fun is that, in their eagerness to please, they will go along with almost anything, observing the rules the dog sets to make sure he always wins. Dogs, as any owner knows, are notoriously poor losers.

Interestingly enough, when dogs play people games, they undergo a profound change in personality. The prospect of matching wits with their owners inspires them to new heights in performance—and surprising bursts of energy.

Most people games consist of three basic forms of exercise, all second nature to dogs, if not to people. These are:

1) Pushing
2) Pulling
3) Running around in circles

See following pages for dogs' favorite people games.

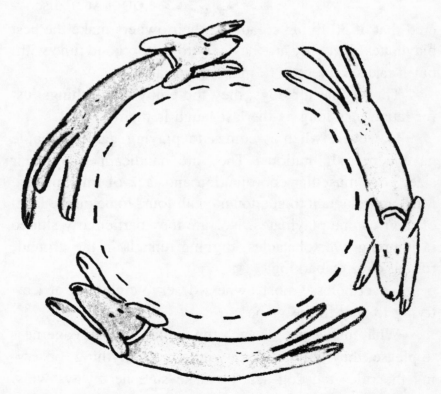

Being able to make a perfect circle is every dog's lifelong ambition.

CATCH ME IF YOU CAN

Objective: To make the dog owner chase after the dog, stumble over furniture and fall on his face.

Play: The players (dog and owner stare at each other, standing several feet apart. Dog barks. At the words ''Will you shut up, please!'' dog cuts loose. Owner follows in pursuit. Play may last from a few minutes to an hour, depending on owner's determination, athletic prowess and physical fitness.

Scoring: First one to slip and fall is the loser.

61

People Game No. 2
MEET ME IN THE DARK

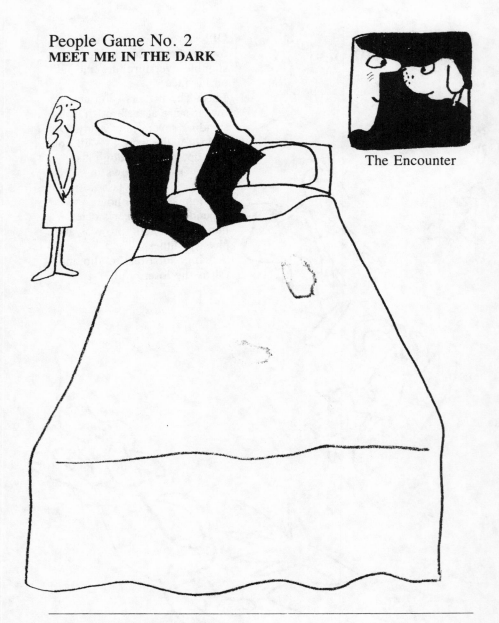

The Encounter

Objective: To mess up the bed.

Play: Dog climbs under the blanket at one end, while owner, looking for him, climbs in at the other. The two meet in the dark under the blanket, nose to nose. Seizing the initiative, dog starts frantically licking owner's face, sending him gasping for air.

Scoring: The one able—and willing—to remain under the blanket wins.

People Game No. 3
SIMON SAYS

Objective: To make the owner work harder than the dog.

Play: This is a great favorite with dogs. While dog sits motionless on the floor rolling his eyes, the leader (owner) gesticulates a series of commands beginning with "I say" or "I want you to . . ." For emphasis, owner may act out the orders before his attentive pet.

Scoring: The game ends when leader discovers a fool has been made of him.

People Game No. 4
WRESTLING

Objective: To show who is the stronger.
Play: In a fit of temper, owner cries, ''I'm gonna get you!'' He moves toward dog, making threatening gestures. The animal draws back, closely watching his opponent's moves. When owner finally grabs dog by the neck, dog throws him to the floor. Standing over the body, dog stops owner from moving, talking and, if fully successful, breathing.
Scoring: He who touches ground with both shoulders loses.

TUG OF WAR*

Objective: To tear apart blankets, towels, sheets and expensive articles of clothing.

Play: Dog grabs the object by one end, growling ominously. Owner is amused, thinking he is still in possession of it. As dog hangs on, owner tries wresting it away from the animal, yanking him back and forth. Game ends when the fabric gives way.

Scoring: The one left holding the larger piece of material is the winner.

* *Grab the pants' leg* is a variation of *tug of war*.

66

People Game No. 6
GET THE SLIPPER

Objective: To tease the owner into believing he has a well-trained animal.

Play: When owner says "Get the slipper," dog takes off and expertly tracks down the slipper. He tears it methodically apart and brings the pieces to the owner, one at a time.

Scoring: Play goes on as long as owner keeps stocking up on slippers.

People Game No. 7
IT IS MINE, IT IS MINE

Objective: To determine ownership.
Play: This game is a variant of "Go fetch!" After owner has thrown the ball, dog retrieves it, actually nudging up against owner's knee, urging him to take it. When owner tries to take the ball, however, dog shakes his head violently, indicating a radical change of mind. With his teeth clenched, only an experienced animal trainer could pry it loose.
Scoring: The one who keeps possession of the ball—i.e., the dog—wins.

People Game No. 8
LIMBO

Objective: To test players' suppleness.
Play: Players wedge themselves into various small spaces—under tables, chairs, bed, dresser, and finally, back of the toilet bowl. The challenge is to keep from touching the objects with any part of the body.
Scoring: Player with the fewest lumps on his head is the winner.

People Game No. 9
TREASURE HUNT

Objective: To collect objects from all around the house.
Play: Dog goes through each room searching for removable items, such as books, shoes, pillows, children's toys and any perishables. All is taken to an undisclosed location.
Scoring: Game ends when there are no more objects to be found.

Objective: To create havoc in the house.

Play: In this game, the roles are reversed. It is the owner who looks for objects hidden by dog. He looks everywhere, mumbling to himself. Most likely places to find hidden objects are chests of drawers, cupboards, flower vases, bathtubs, shelves, filing cabinets, refrigerators and trash cans.

Scoring: Dog gets one point for every unfound item.

Dogs and owners who play together stay together.

MANY DOG OWNERS want to know what toys to buy for their playful pets. The fact is that a dog can amuse himself with any article—as long as he can fit it in his mouth. Since many dogs enjoy biting or even swallowing their toys, they naturally prefer ones that taste good.

For the most part, so-called "dog toys" (i.e., rubber dumbbells, bones and rings) are only for the inexperienced. As with children, a dog, as he grows, needs more sophisticated playthings to pique his intellectual curiosity. Young dogs prefer playing with building blocks, stuffed animals and putty. Later they acquire a taste for tubes of oil paint, home chemistry equipment, electric trains, chess and back-gammon sets.

Round objects have a special appeal to dogs, although no one quite knows why. (It has been speculated that the round shape of the human head accounts for it.) By and large, dogs relish any game or sport that is played with a ball. Given an opportunity, they will make their presence felt in any of the following:

Tennis: Dog will go after a ball in any part of the court, getting there just before the players do.

Golf: Dog will start running after the ball the moment it has been hit. He will then place it in the rough behind the largest tree he can find.

Volleyball: Dog will try nudging the ball out of bounds, making score-keeping a hopeless task.

Pool: Dog will jump on the table and snatch the ball in play, just as it is about to roll into a pocket.

Table tennis: Dog will catch the ball in mid-air and swallow it whole.

ESPECIALLY POPU-
LAR with dogs are people games that involve teaching owners to perform on command. This is usually referred to as "obedience training," and no book on dogs can possibly be complete without it. Dog's approach to obedience training is based on common sense. First, the owner is made to understand who is boss. Once that is settled, the rest is only a matter of patience and long hours of practice.

With regard to following directions, dogs find people fairly intelligent—more so than most other living creatures, with the possible exception of the chimpanzee, the dolphin and, of course, the dog. Here are some of the basic commands humans can be taught to heed:

Walk at heel: When owner walks properly on a lead, it is called "walking at heel" Preferably, he should be made to follow the dog on the right side, never pulling or lagging far behind. Most of all, he must be prevented from making impetuous decisions on his own, such as crossing the street or stopping to take with a friend.

Dogs like to walk
with someone able to
follow directions.
Should the owner
pull too hard, the dog
will exert equal force
going in the oppsoite
way. If this does not
work, the dog will stop
trying altogether and
sit down. Sooner or later
the message will get
through.

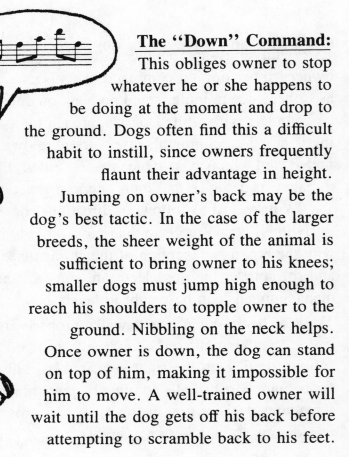

The "Down" Command:

This obliges owner to stop whatever he or she happens to be doing at the moment and drop to the ground. Dogs often find this a difficult habit to instill, since owners frequently flaunt their advantage in height. Jumping on owner's back may be the dog's best tactic. In the case of the larger breeds, the sheer weight of the animal is sufficient to bring owner to his knees; smaller dogs must jump high enough to reach his shoulders to topple owner to the ground. Nibbling on the neck helps. Once owner is down, the dog can stand on top of him, making it impossible for him to move. A well-trained owner will wait until the dog gets off his back before attempting to scramble back to his feet.

Obeying the Call "Come Here": This command is most important since it saves the dog the trouble of exerting himself to reach owner.

To make owner come to dog, all the latter need do is annoy the former. This is never a real problem. The dog can bark, yap, howl, whine or combine all these, preferably off key, or dare his pursuer by leaping up on the furniture, climbing up a bookcase, hiding behind the draperies or simply jumping out the nearest window. The owner will then endeavor to catch him.

Retrieving an Object: Any dog owner can be taught to bring back an object to the dog. First, he must throw it, of course. Having waited in vain for the dog to make the first move, the thrower will give up and bring back the object himself.

ONE OF THE BEST places for people games is inside a car. Since in most states dogs are legally prohibited from driving a motorized vehicle, they are left to look for other ways to amuse themselves.

Some dogs break up the monotony by looking out the window. This involves sticking the head out as far as possible—with someone firmly holding onto the tail if necessary—in the direction of the road ahead. As long as there are interesting roadside attractions, such as garbage dumps, dogs in other cars and McDonald's restaurants, sightseeing can be a stimulating experience. Without these points of interest the dog quickly grows bored. He will then return his attention to his fellow passengers.

The most popular sources of amusement inside the automobile are these:

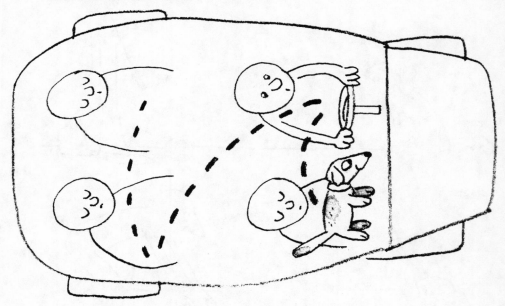

Musical chairs: The idea is to jump from one passenger's lap to another's at brief intervals—say, every two seconds.

Now You See Me, Now You Don't: It is hard to imagine that a good-sized four-legged animal could disappear inside a car, but some dogs have developed an uncanny knack for doing just that. Such dogs can usually be found under the front seat, if owner keeps his eye out for something in the shape of a pancake.

Indoor Hurdle Contest: Dog leaps from back seat to front seat and back again, over the heads and shoulders of his traveling companions.

The Dashboard Daredevil: At first glance, this game appears to be suitable only for small dogs. Not so. Any dog able to stay on top of the dashboard—totally or partially—can play.

Bringing up the Rear: This game is played at the rear window with the nose pressed firmly against the glass and with the body completely blocking the driver's rear view.

Driver's Helper: Dog takes his place at the side or in front of the driver, obstructing his vision of the road ahead. This is a game of chance, fraught with suspense. The odds are about even that the car will crash into an oncoming telephone pole. Same results are likely when the dog sits at the driver's feet, helping him accelerate with his paw.

5

The Guess-Who Game: I Am Not Just a Dog

Though FEW DOGS

have attended acting school, all display an amazing talent for role-playing. They often pretend, and soon come to believe, that they are someone else—much to the confusion of their owner, who might have thought he had a dog for a pet.

The game has interesting possibilities, and it's an easy one to play. Certainly, the modern dog's appearance inspires him to assume a variety of identities. Even a casual glance in the mirror convinces him that any resemblance between his appearance today and that of his ancestors is pure coincidence. The image staring back at him may look like a well-stuffed sausage, a fluffy pillow, a shoebox, a balloon—anything but the savage beast of yesteryear.

No wonder so many modern dogs spend more and more time before the mirror making faces at their reflection and examining themselves from every angle. This preoccupation with themselves has nothing to do with vanity. They are simply—and often rightly so—getting increasingly nervous about their appearance and making plans to change it.

"I AM A BIG DOG."

Every dog dreams of being a different size. Small dogs have delusions of grandeur, and big dogs often ponder how it would feel to be a cuddly parlor pet.

84

A room left behind by a playful Great Dane who thought he was a
Chihuahua.

The "Hey, I am a cat" game. To many dogs, the fact that cats are treated with more respect is a shocking affront. Cats are lifted off the floor more readily and never by the scruff of the neck; they are given preferential treatment on couches and laps; they are not forced to take baths; and their disobedience is often tolerated—even praised—as a sign of an independent spirit.

Purring like a contented cat is one way to let owner know the dog in his lap is actually a member of the feline family.

Rubbing against people's legs is another ploy used by dogs endeavoring to be cats. Again, their performance does not always carry conviction.

88

Showing off the trophy brings a mixed response from the audience.

Landing softly on all fours like a cat is every dog's secret ambition. Very rarely does he land on all fours and never without a resounding thud.

Cathouse is better than doghouse—it offers a superior view. Moreover, sitting above the ground allows dog to look down at his owner.

89

And if I am not a cat, then . . .

"I am a bird. I can fly through open spaces with my ears as airfoils."

"I am a rabbit. No one can catch me."

"I am a moth. I can chew holes in wool sweaters and socks. Mothballs are among my favorite condiments."

"I am a nightingale. When it comes to singing, whose voice can compare to mine?"

"I am a bear. In the summer, I sleep most of the time. In the winter, I sleep all the time."

"I am a pig. I eat just as much —and as noisily."

It SHOULD be clear from the above that dogs indulge in a healthy amount of wishful thinking.

This is also demonstrated by their actions.

It appears that dogs are especially fond of fantasizing that they live in a world in which they are no longer treated as second-class citizens.

Imagine . . . in this utopia, they would never again be discriminated against. All "No Dogs Allowed" signs would be eliminated. Landlords would be compelled to rent apartments to people with dogs, or even dogs with people. Dogs would be welcomed in supermarkets to pick up items for themselves outside the pet-food section. They would be served meals three to five times a day, with time out for snacks in between. Refrigerator doors would be designed so any dog can open them. Automobiles would come fully equipped with cushioned seats designed exclusively for them. All fire hydrants would be designated permanent landmarks.

"I am human. Even more so than my master. I love to watch television. Of all programs, my favorite are dog-food commercials."

6

Games City Dogs Play: The Canine Urbanite

It IS SAID that city living is confining, giving those who live there little room to maneuver. This is pure nonsense as far as dogs are concerned. Who needs to go anywhere when there is an unoccupied cushion on the living-room couch?

The fact is that in the city dogs have a chance to live more graciously than anywhere else. Amenities abound, and many are designed to accommodate basic needs. For example, it is not uncommon to find four or five fire hydrants on a single block within easy walking distance of each other.

Where there are no fire hydrants, a gamut of other public facilities are at the dog's disposal. There is scarcely a limit to the array of trees, store entrances, parking meters and sides of parked cars available to fastidious canines.

Then, of course, there are the parks. These verdant islands of tranquility exist principally for one reason: to provide a gathering place for all dogs of the city, giving them a chance to commune with nature. Dogs like parks. Here they can meet their peers, talk things over and settle differences of opinion.

Another good place for friendly social encounters is the elevator.

Popular with city dogs is a pastime referred to as "going for a walk." This game is always good for a few laughs. As long as owner holds on, there is little chance he can go anywhere without the dog's consent. There are many ways to play the game, and the outcome is always the same. The dog wins.

One version is called "I fooled you, didn't I?" Here is how this game is played. Dog expresses keen interest in going outdoors. The moment the leash is fastened to his collar, he makes a dash for it, dragging his master's body to the door. A fast reconnaissance of the territory and the dog indicates his desire to turn around and go home. The logic of all this often escapes dog owners. But not the dog. Common sense tells him that with the inspection of all appropriate fire hydrants, trees and other markings, any further strolling about is no longer worthy of his attention.

Leash wrapped around owner's legs will effectively prevent him from straying.

Two dogs on a leash can create an even more knotty situation.

98

It is said that taking a dog for a walk is good exercise. So it is—for the owner.

Sometimes an irresistible force can turn a dog into an immovable object.

Going around the tree faster
than owner produces an
interesting dilemma.

Climbing over and under things
gives dog endless opportunities
to make owner wish he had
stayed home.

100

Is your dog a traffic stopper?

The city dog's favorite perch is at the window. From here he can watch the world go by—and with minimum effort. There is so much to see.

103

And there is even more to smell
—even with his eyes closed.

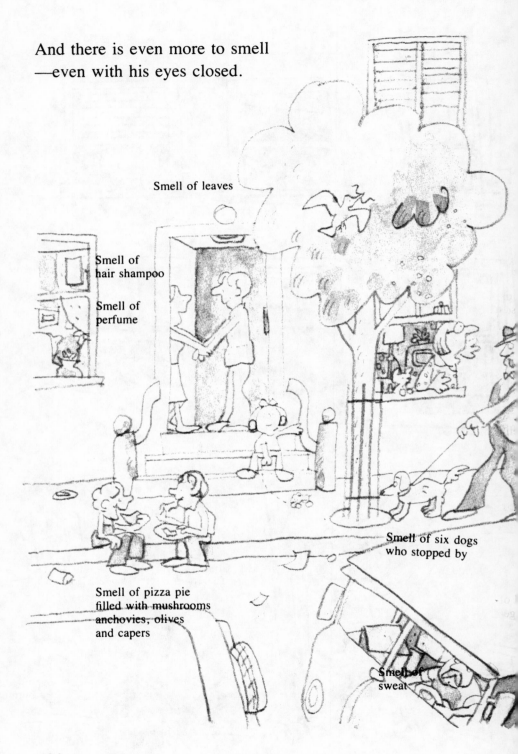

Smell of leaves

Smell of
hair shampoo

Smell of
perfume

Smell of six dogs
who stopped by

Smell of pizza pie
filled with mushrooms
anchovies, olives
and capers

Smell of
sweat

104

105

For the sake of companionship, many owners feel compelled to drag their pet along with them wherever they go. There are times when dogs are quite agreeable.

107

And there are times when they are not.

Remember: Dogs don't like to be left behind.

ABOUT ONE THING there can be no question: The life of a city dog is more complex than that of his country cousin.

For one thing, the city is more crowded. For reasons not easily understood, dogs are mandated by law to take their owners with them when going for a walk and to make sure he is safely curbed at all times. This inevitably imposes certain limitations on the dog's freedom of mobility.

For another thing, a dog's life in a metropolitan area is more competitive. There are thousands of other dogs— equally qualified—trying to eke out a living just as he is. And that's not all. There are those who actually think dogs are less important than people.

Thus, the city dog has his own set of problems which he must face up to. Like his forefathers thousands of years ago, he too is surrounded by natural enemies. Only the faces have changed; now they come on with a forced smile.

Natural Enemy No. 1: The Sign Painter

Natural Enemy No. 2: The Garbage Collector

Natural Enemy No. 3: The Dog Trainer

Natural Enemy No. 4: The Restaurant Owner

111

As A RULE, urban dogs are more clothes-conscious than dogs living outside the city limits, especially when appearing in public. They accept this as part of sophisticated living. In polite society, public displays of nudity are looked upon askance.

Most dogs do not mind wearing the latest fashion; they know that clothes often make the dog. They dress for each other, not for people. A dog can rely on his smell up close, but from a distance he knows that it is appearance that counts.

Here is what fashionable dogs of today wear on a city street:

113

All this is not to suggest, of course, that city dogs have time on their hands. They maintain a demanding schedule, making full use of the cultural advantages offered by a metropolitan environment.

Here is a typical day in the life of a canine urbanite:

6-6:05 AM	Wakes to the rattle of a garbage truck picking up a load in front of building. Goes to the window to take a good look, then returns to his station between his master and mistress.
7-7:10	Wakes to the sound of human voices coming from the adjoining apartment. The neighbors are at it again. Accustomed to that sort of noise, dog goes back to sleep.
7:30	Wakes as owner gets up to take a shower, sweeping him off the bed. Taking a pillow in his teeth, dog establishes temporary residence under the bed.
8:00	When his master leaves the room, he promptly climbs back up on the bed.
9:00	Again he is awakened, this time by his mistress insisting she cannot make the bed as long as he is on it. To avoid a confrontation, dog tunnels under the blanket. Mistress responds by pulling him out by the tail, calling dog names other than his own.
9:10	Taking it all in stride, dog elects to continue his nap on the living-room couch.
9:20	The smells of toast, scrambled eggs and hot cereal drift by his nose. Slowly opening his eyes, he heads in the general direction of the kitchen for breakfast.

10:00	He accompanies his mistress to the supermarket to supervise the selection of dog food.
10:40	On the way home, he encounters another dog on the street, larger than he. He growls.
10:45	Other dog lifts him off the ground by the ear. The two are separated by their owners.
10:50	He continues on his way. At the entrance to the apartment building, he bares his teeth at the doorman. Doorman insults him. As the dog retaliates by tearing the doorman's trousers, he is kicked unceremoniously in the snout.
10:55	Owner hands doorman thirty dollars to defray the cost of a new pair of pants, thus settling the matter out of court. The placated doorman reciprocates by calling the animal a "nice little dog" and unmindful of the consequences, pats him on the head.
10:56	Dog takes doorman's fingers in his mouth.
11:00	Owner gives doorman a blank check to cover medical expenses.
11:10	Dog now is told by his owner that he is a "bad, bad, bad dog." Utterly mystified, he listens as if he were hearing it for the first time.
11:20	Safe in the apartment, dog immediately takes to the bedroom for a moment of reflection. Later that day, at 6:30 PM, Dog's sleep is interrupted by the odor—now of fried chicken—emanating from the dining area.
6:31 PM	He presents himself at the dining table, ready for dinner.
7:36	He follows mistress to the kitchen sink to take care of the leftovers.

115

8:00	Along with the family, he watches television.
8:10	Bored by the program, dog goes back to the bedroom to prepare for bedtime.
8:11	With a sigh, he falls asleep exhausted after a full day.

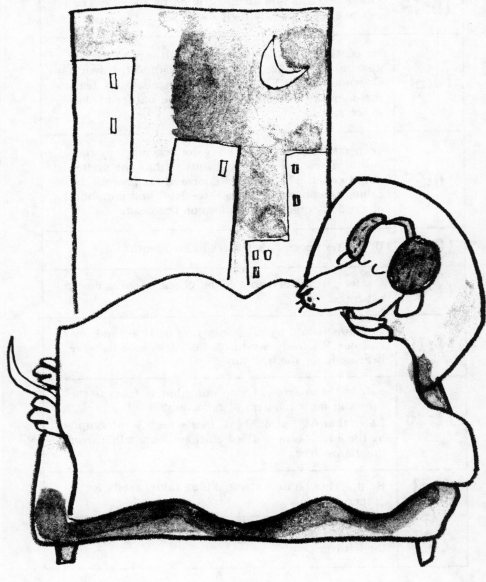

7

Games Country Dogs Play: A Wide-Open World

Fewer FIRE HYDRANTS

dot the landscape, but still there is enough to do outside the city to keep a dog occupied.

For one thing, every country dog must spend a good part of his time on such routine matters as defending his territory—even more threatened here than in the city. Dogs seem to pop out from everywhere; from houses, garages, hedgerows, treehouses, garbage cans, and mailboxes. In most suburbs, dogs seem to outnumber people about three to one. Unlike city dogs, they move around freely and drop in on each other for social visits whenever the mood strikes —which is all the time.

A major problem is that even country and suburban dogs have trouble defining the boundaries—and location— of their territory, as hard as they may try. Not all lots are surrounded by a fence. And even if they were, such lines of demarcation have no meaning to a dog making his appointed rounds.

Perhaps this is why so much of the country dog owner's time is spent looking for his dog. The search usually begins in the evening when he returns from work to hear from his family that one of the members has once again disappeared.

119

Phone calls follow to neighbors living in the immediate and not so immediate vicinity. The answer is always the same. No, nobody has seen the dog. The next question then usually comes from the other end of the line: Has the caller by any chance seen *their* dog—easily recognizable by his drooping ears, more or less white coat, black markings above the eyes, etc., etc.

It is rare, however, that the dog will not eventually return. Having been booted out everywhere else, he makes his choice by a simple process of elimination.

Homes in the country are more vulnerable to attack than those in the city. And so the canine occupant must be continually on the alert. He must not for a minute let his guard down. It is his responsibility to strike terror into anything of suspicious nature, such as a passing school bus, delivery truck or, for that matter, anything that moves. He can let his presence be known by simply barking for several minutes or hours. Rarely will his cry of alarm go unheeded.

As common courtesy, all other dogs in the neighborhood will instantly join in. Barking is the hallmark of an accomplished watchdog; the possessor of such a dog, it is said, owns something as valuable as a burglar alarm, except that the latter can be turned off.

Long-distance duets, of course, are not limited to other dogs only. Two-part harmonies can be improvised with anything that makes noise and at any hour of the day—or night. Dogs have been known to answer bullfrogs' mating calls, farm animals braying, telephones ringing, tree branches falling, tires screeching, toilets flushing or the voice of someone singing in the shower down the road. Since the sound of music is particularly pleasing to canine ears, there is a good chance the dog will try his best to harmonize. All dogs have a high opinion of their musical talents, which they consider much superior—and certainly more pleasing to the ear—to that of humans.

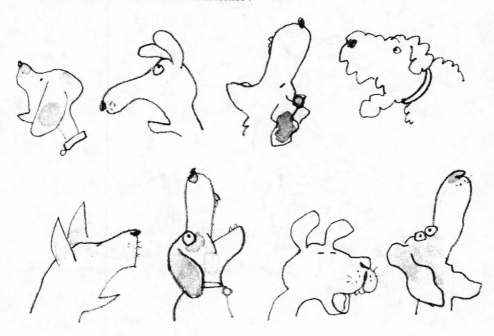

The preceding is not to suggest that a well-trained watchdog barks indiscriminately at anything or anybody who happens to be around. Clearly, his finely honed instinct allows him to distinguish between friend and foe, and he will react accordingly.

The Mailman

Those shown on these pages are among the country dog's greatest natural enemies. He will do his best to discourage them from encroaching on what he considers his exclusive territory.

The Delivery Man

The Baby-sitter　　　　　　　　　**The Electrician**

The Plumber

The Gardener

Then, of course, there are those to whom dogs take an immediate liking. They will see to it that these people feel right at home.

Door-to-Door Salesman

Wife's Lover

Outlaws

I nothing else, living in the country offers the dog plenty of room to check out new territories. He can roam freely without having owner following in his footsteps. Few obstacles stand in his way. Fences can be scaled or tunneled under, flower beds can be demolished on the run, swimming pool can be crossed, and it is a relatively simple matter to bo around people who are trying to stop him. The typical running track of a country dog—his daily constitutional as it were—may look something like this.

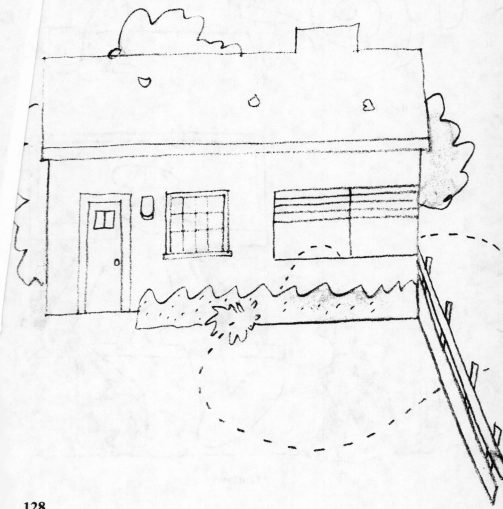

Free of constant supervision, the dog at last can pursue his personal interests, the most important of which is chasing. He can chase above the ground, under the ground, along the ground, in water and in the air.

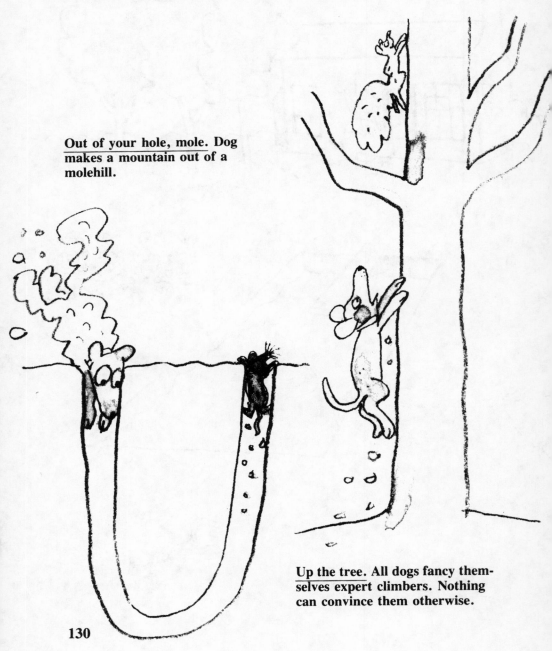

Out of your hole, mole. Dog makes a mountain out of a molehill.

Up the tree. All dogs fancy themselves expert climbers. Nothing can convince them otherwise.

Underwater chase. Some dogs will risk anything to catch their prey. This is one of the best ways—or often the only way—to get dogs to bathe.

I'll get you, bird. Dog leaves ground. Bird flies off, chuckling to itself. Dog lands on his side.

Run, rabbit, run. Flower beds make an ideal track for a race between a swift dog and an even swifter rabbit.

131

"Follow that car" is another form of chase, designed to amuse the dog, if not the driver. The game begins with the dog lying low in ambush at his observation post, usually behind a bush. Sighting the car, he inches closer to the road, ready for the attack. As the vehicle approaches, he attacks, leaping high in the air. Trying to avert a collision, the driver steers his car off the road, up the sidewalk and finally—after crushing a mailbox—back to the street. At this point, dog calmly returns to his starting point to await the next unsuspecting driver.

To a dog, being chased is almost as much fun as chasing. This game is played once again to prove the dog's unquestionable physical—and, of course, mental—superiority over human beings.

Having nothing better to do, most country dogs will accept their master's invitation to join him on a hunting trip. They appreciate the fact that while hunting may constitute an interruption of their daily routine, it is still a far cry from what their forebears had to do. The modern dog must do little more than retrieve the quarry after it has been done in by his master. Knowing what is expected from them, many dogs will go so far as to feign interest in the proceedings.

Here is the day of a dog accompanying his master on a duck hunt.

4:00 AM	Alarm clock rings. Both master and dog go back to sleep.
4:30	Alarm clock rings. Both the master and dog go back to sleep.
6:30	Master gets up.

7–7:30	Dog gets up.
8:00–10:00	Dog yawns and catches up with his lost sleep on the front seat of car.
10:15	Hunter takes position in the duck blind waiting for confrontation. Dog rolls over to his side and dreams about <u>caneton aux pêches</u>.
2:30 PM	The birds arrive.
2:32	Hunter takes aim and downs one.
2:35	Dog retrieves game and receives hunter's effusive praises.
2:36–2:40	Dog wags his tail.
3:00	Both go back to car for lunch of sandwiches.
3:30–5:30	Return home. Dog recuperates on couch.
7:30–8:30	Wife prepares the duck, following dog's favorite recipe. Supper follows.
9:00	While hunter excitedly describes the hunt, dog calls it a day.

And here is a typical day of deer hunting with a dog for a companion.

5:30 AM	The hunter rises and dons his Day-Glo-red hunting jacket and cap, bright enough to cause dog to blink and rise to his feet.
6:30– 10:00	Drive to the hunting ground.
10:05	Both settle on a hillside. Dog goes to sleep.
11:25	Wind carries scent of deer to the dog, and he opens an eye.

11:26	He opens both eyes.
11:27	He barks.
11:28	"Where, where?" asks his master.
11:45	With the help of his dog, the hunter finally sights the deer.
11:46	He shoots.
11:47	He misses. Deer bounds away and disappears.
11:48	"Son of a ——," the hunter blurts, checking himself just in time from giving offense to his companion.
11:49	Dog goes to sleep.
2:45 PM	Both move to another spot.
3:10	Dog is again awakened. He barks.
3:11	Hunter shoots and misses the deer.
4:30	Both move to another spot.
5:10	Dog wakes up and barks.

5:11	Hunter shoots and misses the deer.
5:45	The hunter drives to a nearby bar and buys the carcass of a six-pointer from the local plumber.
6:00– 9:30	They drive home, deer on the roof.
9:35	Wife and kids admire the trophy.
9:40	Dog retires while his master tells everyone how he shot the deer.

Another source of excitement for outdoor dogs is fishing. They don't mind this activity because (1) as in hunting, they like the idea that catching fish no longer involves effort on their part, and (2) they approve of the taste—baked, fried, marinated or steamed.

Here is the day of a dog acting as a fishing companion:

7:00 AM	Alarm clock rings. Master gets up.
7:30	Dog sleepwalks to the car.
8:00– 9:15	Drive to the dock and board the boat. Dog goes back to sleep, ignoring the roar of the outboard motor.
9:20	Master turns off the engine and casts for fish.
10:30	Master says, "They aren't biting today."

1:45 PM	Master says, "Not biting today at all."
4:30	Master finally catches a small bass and shows it to his companion. Dog sniffs politely at the fish.
4:31	Dog helps himself to some worms in the bait bucket while his master casts again.
5:00– 6:15	They drive home.
7:00	Master reminisces with family about all the fish that got away. Dog keeps his opinion to himself, trying to maintain a low profile.
7:05	Wife suddenly remembers the fresh fish she bought that morning for dinner. Everyone approves, including the dog.
7:15– 8:30	Master continues to reminisce about his day while the family and dog watch television.
8:30– 9:00	Lemon sole with almonds for dinner.
9:30	His appetite satisfied, dog retires to the bedroom.

8

You Can Tell a Breed by the Games He Plays

Breeds NOT ONLY look

different, varying in size, weight and facial expression; each breed plays its own special set of games. The rules of these games are passed down from generation to generation, with each new player adding refinements, but always careful not to go against established traditions.

Often, one breed will invite another to join in the fun— with disconcerting results. Even when the spirit of cooperation prevails and playmates manage to get along for several minutes without a fight, it can be a trying experience for, say, a dachshund to enter a running contest with a whippet, for a Chihuahua to wrestle a Newfoundland or for the mute Basenji to try outbaying a beagle.

Of all playing partners, the best are still owners, who will do just about anything to please their dog. Here the outcome depends in large part on the owner's disposition. Some people turn out to be spoilsports—refusing to climb under beds, get down on all fours, jump on top of tables or out the window.

However, it should be pointed out once again that such spoilsports are an exception to the rule. Most people earnestly try to play along, until they drop to the ground. For their part, most dogs show their appreciation by giving the owner enough time to catch his breath and get back on his feet before resuming the fun.

What follows are the favorite games of breeds. The listing is alphabetical to avoid injuring the feelings of various breed owners and, more importantly, of the breeds themselves.

BASSET HOUND

Minimum speed: a slow two miles an hour. Maximum speed: a fast two miles an hour. Swift acceleration causes his coat to flap in the wind.

BEAGLE

He takes his domestic responsibilities very seriously. Especially when it comes to protecting what is rightfully his.

BEDLINGTON TERRIER

Can see no reason why a dog must look like a dog. Why not a lamb?

BICHON FRISE

He knows just how cute he is. So he graciously lends his much needed services as a decorative accent to sofas, beds, comfortable chairs and other select places around the home. All he asks for in exchange is that you cater to his every whim.

BOSTON TERRIER

Caution: noisy sleeper. Requires bedmates with high tolerance level. Or earplugs.

BULLDOG

Some people say dogs and their owners often look alike. Opposites attract. But the best friends often have a lot in common.

CHIHUAHUA

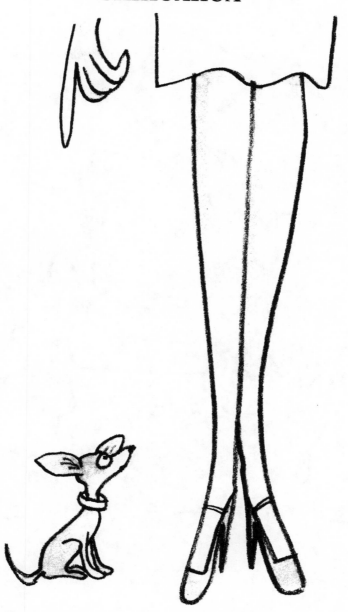

No dog can make you feel as important as a Chihuahua. At the
sound of your command, his ears shoot up as if standing at attention.
This makes it easier for the sound to travel in one ear and out the
other.

CHOW CHOW

They say the Chow Chow's very presence commands respect. No one knows that better than the Chow Chow.

152

COCKER SPANIEL

Fetching comes naturally to this dog. So does making you feel guilty for letting him work so hard.

COLLIE

He likes to watch television. He particularly admires performers who save drowning children, scale vertical mountains, open locked doors, leap from rooftops of burning buildings and make a lot of money.

DACHSHUND

He is the envy of other dogs. The average house or apartment is full of hiding places just right for avoiding the solicitous attentions of human beings.

DALMATIAN

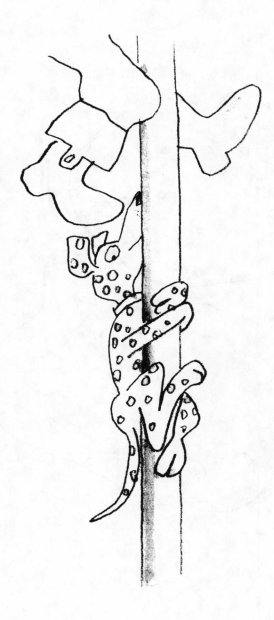

Some dogs chase trucks. The smart ones ride on them and chase fires.

DOBERMAN

He takes great pride in his work. In fact, he is so dedicated that he won't stand for any interruptions.

FOX TERRIER

Wild agitation of the hindquarters is the Fox Terrier's reaction to the sight of his owner. A classic example of the tail wagging the dog.

GERMAN SHEPHERD

His sensitive nose makes him an invaluable member of law-enforcement teams. The German Shepherd likes his work. In fact, he is very high on it.

GREAT DANE

Some people confuse the Great Dane with a small horse. This adds immeasurably to his self-image. Far be it from him to clarify the matter.

GREYHOUND

He is one of the swiftest animals alive. The only animal who seems consistently to outdistance a Greyhound is another Greyhound.

TERRIERS

There are many kinds of Terriers, and all share the ability to turn your home into a one-ring circus. And keep in mind that their acrobatic feats are not just for show.

MALTESE

He makes up in speed what he lacks in size. It is even rumored that the jogging craze started with owners walking their Maltese.

PEKINGESE

Lack of height hardly deters the Pekingese from looking down his nose at the rest of the world. Human beings are no exception.

POINTER

His natural instinct comes in handy in a variety of situations.

POODLE

It is true that Poodles are among the most playful of pets. Their creativity in inventing new games never ceases to amaze their owners.

166

SCHNAUZER

This dog is known for his fearless disposition, daredevil antics and raw courage. But not for his common sense.

ST. BERNARD

He knows how to hold his liquor.

MUTT

Due to his lack of pedigree, the Mutt is totally unpredictable in his gamesmanship. Anything goes.

THE END